Christopher Columbus
And The New World of His Discovery
Volume 5

FILSON YOUNG
[ZHINGOORA BOOKS]

About Author

Alexander Bell Filson Young was a journalist, BBC programme advisor and author. His wrote the book on Titanic, a RMS Titanic ship. His famous works includeTitanic, The Relief of Mafekingand etc.

DESPERATE REMEDIES

CHAPTER I

THE VOYAGE TO CUBA

The sight of the greater part of their fleet disappearing in the direction of home threw back the unstable Spanish colony into doubt and despondency. The brief encouragement afforded by Ojeda's report soon died away, and the actual discomforts of life in Isabella were more important than visionary luxuries that seemed to recede into the distance with the vanishing ships. The food supply was the cause of much discomfort; the jobbery and dishonesty which seem inseparable from the fitting out of a large expedition had stored the ships with bad wine and imperfectly cured provisions; and these combined with the unhealthy climate to produce a good deal of sickness. The feeling against Columbus, never far below the Spanish surface, began to express itself definitely in treacherous consultations and plots; and these were fomented by Bernal Diaz, the comptroller of the colony, who had access to Columbus's papers and had seen the letter sent by him to Spain. Columbus was at this time prostrated by an attack of fever, and Diaz took the opportunity to work the growing discontent up to the point of action. He told the colonists that Columbus had painted their condition in far too favourable terms; that he was deceiving them as well as the Sovereigns; and a plot was hatched to seize the ships that remained and sail for home, leaving Columbus behind to enjoy the riches that he had falsely boasted about. They were ready to take alarm at anything, and to believe anything one way or the other; and as they had believed Ojeda when he came back with his report of riches, now they believed Cado, the assayer, who said that even such gold as had been found was of a very poor and worthless quality. The mutiny developed fast; and a table of charges against Columbus, which was to be produced in Spain as a justification for it, had actually been drawn up when the Admiral, recovering from his illness, discovered what was on foot. He dealt promptly and firmly with it in his quarterdeck manner, which was always far more effective than his viceregal manner. Diaz was imprisoned and lodged in chains on board one of the ships, to be sent to Spain for trial; and the other ringleaders were punished also according to their deserts. The guns and ammunition were all stored together on one ship under a safe guard, and the mutiny was stamped out. But the Spaniards did not love Columbus any the better for it; did not any the more easily forgive him for being in command of them and for being a foreigner.

But it would never do for the colony to stagnate in Isabella, and Columbus decided to make a serious attempt, not merely to discover the gold of Cibao, but to get it. He therefore organised a military expedition of about 400 men, including artificers, miners, and carriers, with the little cavalry force that had been brought out from Spain. Every one who had armour wore it, flags and banners were carried, drums and trumpets were sounded; the horses were decked out in rich caparisons, and as glittering and formidable a show was made as possible. Leaving his brother James in command of the settlement, Columbus set out on the 12th of March to the interior of the island. Through the forest and up the mountainside a road was cut by pioneers from among the aristocratic adventurers who had come with the party; which road, the first made in the New World, was called El Puerto de los Hidalgos. The formidable, glittering cavalcade inspired the natives with terror and amazement; they had never seen horses before, and when one of the soldiers dismounted it seemed to them as though some terrifying two-headed, six-limbed beast had come asunder. What with their fright of the horses and their desire to possess the trinkets that were carried they were very friendly and hospitable, and supplied the expedition with plenty of food. At last, after passing mountain ranges that made their hearts faint, and rich valleys that made them hopeful again, the explorers came to the mountains of Cibao, and passing over the first range found themselves in a little valley at the foot of the hills where a river wound round a fertile plain and there was ample accommodation for an encampment. There were the usual signs of gold, and Columbus saw in the brightly coloured stones of the river-bed evidence of unbounded wealth in precious stones. At last he had come to the place! He who had doubted so much, and whose faith had wavered, had now been led to a place where he could touch and handle the gold and jewels of his desire; and he therefore called the place Saint Thomas. He built a fort here, leaving a garrison of fifty-six men under the command of Pedro Margarite to collect gold from the natives, and himself returned to Isabella, which he reached at the end of March.

Enforced absence from the thing he has organised is a great test of efficiency in any man. The world is full of men who can do things themselves; but those who can organise from the industry of their men a machine which will steadily perform the work whether the organiser is absent or present are rare indeed. Columbus was one of the first class. His own power and personality generally gave him some kind of mastery over any circumstances in which he was immediately concerned; but let him be absent for a little time, and his organisation went to pieces. No one was better than he at conducting a one-man concern; and his conduct of the first voyage, so long as he had his company under his immediate command, was a model of efficiency. But when the material under his command began to grow and to be divided into groups his life became a succession of ups and downs. While he was settling and disciplining one group mutiny and disorder would attack the other; and when he went to attend to them, the first one immediately fell into confusion again. He dealt with the discontent in Isabella, organising the better disposed part of it in productive labour, and himself marching the malcontents into something like discipline and order, leaving them at Saint Thomas, as we have seen, usefully collecting gold. But while he was away the people at Isabella had got themselves into trouble again, and when he arrived there on the morning of March 29th he found the town in a deplorable condition. The lake beside which the city had been built, and which seemed so attractive and healthy a spot, turned out to be nothing better than a fever trap. Drained from the malarial marshes, its sickly exhalations soon produced an epidemic that incapacitated more than half the colony and interrupted the building operations. The time of those who were well was entirely occupied with the care of those who were sick, and all productive work was at a standstill. The reeking virgin soil had produced crops in an incredibly short time, and the sowings of January were ready for reaping in the beginning of April. But there was no one to reap them, and the further cultivation of the ground had necessarily been neglected.

The faint-hearted Spaniards, who never could meet any trouble without grumbling, were now in the depths of despair and angry discontent; and it had not pleased them to be put on a short allowance of even the unwholesome provisions that remained from the original store. A couple of rude hand-mills had been erected for the making of flour, and as food was the first necessity Columbus immediately put all the able-bodied men in the colony, whatever their rank, to the elementary manual work of grinding. Friar Buil and the twelve Benedictine brothers who were with him thought this a wise order, assuming of course that as clerics they would not be asked to work. But great was their astonishment, and loud and angry their criticism of the Admiral, when they found that they also were obliged to labour with their hands. But Columbus was firm; there were absolutely no exceptions made; hidalgo and priest had to work alongside of sailor and labourer; and the curses of the living mingled with those of the dying on the man whose boastful words had brought them to such a place and such a condition.

It was only in the nature of things that news should now arrive of trouble at Saint Thomas. Gold and women again; instead of bartering or digging, the Spaniards had been stealing; and discipline had been relaxed, with the usual disastrous results with regard to the women of the adjacent native tribes. Pedro Margarite sent a nervous message to Columbus expressing his fear that Caonabo, the native king, should be exasperated to the point of attacking them again. Columbus therefore despatched

Ojeda in command of a force of 350 armed men to Saint Thomas with instructions that he was to take over the command of that post, while Margarite was to take out an expedition in search of Caonabo whom, with his brothers, Margarite was instructed to capture at all costs.

Having thus set things going in the interior, and once more restored Isabella to something like order, he decided to take three ships and attempt to discover the coast of Cathay. The old Nina, the San Juan, and the Cordera, three small caravels, were provisioned for six months and manned by a company of fifty-two men. Francisco Nino went once more with the Admiral as pilot, and the faithful Juan de la Cosa was taken to draw charts; one of the monks also, to act as chaplain. The Admiral had a steward, a secretary, ten seamen and six boys to complete the company on the Nina. The San Juan was commanded by Alonso Perez Roldan and the Cordera by Christoval Nino. Diego was again left in command of the colony, with four counsellors, Friar Buil, Fernandez Coronel, Alonso Sanchez Carvajal, and Juan de Luxan, to assist his authority.

The Admiral sailed on April 24th, steering to the westward and touching at La Navidad before he bore away to the island of Cuba, the southern shore of which it was now his intention to explore. At one of his first anchorages he discovered a native feast going on, and when the boats from his ships pulled ashore the feasters fled in terror—the hungry Spaniards finishing their meal for them. Presently, however, the feasters were induced to come back, and Columbus with soft speeches made them a compensation for the food that had been taken, and produced a favourable impression, as his habit was; with the result that all along the coast he was kindly received by the natives, who supplied him with food and fresh fruit in return for trinkets. At the harbour now known as Santiago de Cuba, where he anchored on May 2nd, he had what seemed like authentic information of a great island to the southward which was alleged to be the source of all the gold. The very compasses of Columbus's ships seem by this time to have become demagnetised, and to have pointed only to gold; for no sooner had he heard this report than he bore away to the south in pursuit of that faint yellow glitter that had now quite taken the place of the original inner light of faith.

The low coast of Jamaica, hazy and blue at first, but afterwards warming into a golden belt crowned by the paler and deeper greens of the foliage, was sighted first by Columbus on Sunday, May 4th; and he anchored the next day in the beautiful harbour of Saint Anne, to which he gave the name of Santa Gloria. To the island itself he gave the name of Santiago, which however has never displaced its native name of Jamaica. The dim blue mountains and clumps of lofty trees about the bay were wonderful even to Columbus, whose eyes must by this time have been growing accustomed to the beauty of the West Indies, and he lost his heart to Jamaica from the first moment that his eyes rested on its green and golden shores. Perhaps he was by this time a little out of conceit with Hayti; but be that as it may he retracted all the superlatives he had ever used for the other lands of his discovery, and bestowed them in his heart upon Jamaica.

He was not humanly so well received as he had been on the other islands, for when he cast anchor the natives came out in canoes threatening hostilities and had to be appeased with red caps and hawks' bells. Next day, however, Columbus wished to careen his ships, and sailed a little to the west until he found a suitable beach at Puerto Bueno; and as he approached the shore some large canoes filled with painted and feathered warriors came out and attacked his ships, showering arrows and javelins, and whooping and screaming at the Spaniards. The guns were discharged, and an armed party sent ashore in a boat, and the natives were soon put to flight. There was no renewal of hostilities; the next day the local cacique came down offering provisions and help; presents were exchanged, and cordial relations established. Columbus noticed that the Jamaicans seemed to be a much more virile community than either the Cubans or the people of Espanola. They had enormous canoes hollowed out of single mahogany trees, some of them 96 feet long and 8 feet broad, which they handled with the greatest ease and dexterity; they had a merry way with them too, were quick of apprehension and clever at expressing their meaning, and in their domestic utensils and implements they showed an advance in civilisation on the other islanders of the group. Columbus did some trade with the islanders as he sailed along the coast, but he does not seem to have believed much in the gold story, for after sailing to the western point of the island he bore away to the north again and sighted the coast of Cuba on the 18th of May.

The reason why Columbus kept returning to the coast of Cuba was that he believed it to be the mainland of Asia. The unlettered natives, who had never read Marco Polo, told him that it was an island, although no man had ever seen the end of it; but Columbus did not believe them, and sailed westward in the belief that he would presently come upon the country and city of Cathay. Soon he found himself in the wonderful labyrinth of islets and sandbanks off the south coast; and because of the wonderful colours of their flowers and climbing plants he called them Jardin de la Reina or Queen's Garden. Dangerous as the navigation through these islands was, he preferred to risk the shoals and sandbanks rather than round them out at sea to the southward, for he believed them to be the islands which, according to Marco Polo, lay in masses along the coast of Cathay. In this adventure he had a very hard time of it; the lead had to be used all the time, the ships often had to be towed, the wind veered round from every quarter of the compass, and there were squalls and tempests, and currents that threatened to set them ashore. By great good fortune, however, they managed to get through the Archipelago without mishap. By June 3rd they were sailing along the coast again, and Columbus had some conversation with an old cacique who told him of a province called Mangon (or so Columbus understood him) that lay to the west. Sir John Mandeville had described the province of Mangi as being the richest in Cathay; and of course, thought the Admiral, this must be the place. He went westward past the Gulf of Xagua and got into the shallow sandy waters, now known as the Jardinillos Bank, where the sea was whitened with particles of sand. When he had got clear of this shoal water he stood across a broad bay towards a native settlement where he was able to take in yams, fruit, fish, and fresh water.

But this excitement and hard work were telling on the Admiral, and when a native told him that there was a tribe close by with long tails, he believed him; and later, when one of his men, coming back from a shore expedition, reported that he had seen some figures in a forest wearing white robes, Columbus believed that they were the people with the tails, who wore a long garment to conceal them.

He was moving in a world of enchantment; the weather was like no weather in any known part of the world; there were fogs, black and thick, which blew down suddenly from the low marshy land, and blew away again as suddenly; the sea was sometimes white as milk, sometimes black as pitch, sometimes purple, sometimes green; scarlet cranes stood looking at them as they slid past the low sandbanks; the warm foggy air smelt of roses; shoals of turtles covered the waters, black butterflies circled in the mist; and the fever that was beginning to work in the Admiral's blood mounted to his brain, so that in this land of bad dreams his fixed ideas began to dominate all his other faculties, and he decided that he must certainly be on the coast of Cathay, in the magic land described by Marco Polo.

There is nothing which illustrates the arbitrary and despotic government of sea life so well as the nautical phrase "make it so." The very hours of the day, slipping westward under the keel of an east-going ship, are "made" by rigid decree; the captain takes his observation of sun or stars, and announces the position of the ship to be at a certain spot on the surface of the globe; any errors of judgment or deficiencies of method are covered by the words "make it so." And in all the elusive phenomena surrounding him the fevered brain of the Admiral discerned evidence that he was really upon the coast of Asia, although there was no method by which he could place the matter beyond a doubt. The word Asia was not printed upon the sands of Cuba, as it might be upon a map; the lines of longitude did not lie visibly across the surface of the sea; there was nothing but sea and land, the Admiral's charts, and his own conviction. Therefore Columbus decided to "make it so." If there was no other way of being sure that this was the coast of Cathay, he would decree it to be the coast of Cathay by a legal document and by oaths and affidavits. He would force upon the members of his expedition a conviction at least equal to his own; and instead of pursuing any further the coast that stretched interminably west and south-west, he decided to say, in effect, and once and for all, "Let this be the mainland of Asia."

He called his secretary to him and made him draw up a form of oath or testament, to which every member of the expedition was required to subscribe, affirming that the land off which they were then lying (12th June 1494), was the mainland of the Indies and that it was possible to return to Spain by land from that place; and every officer who should ever deny it in the future was laid under a penalty of ten thousand maravedis, and every ship's boy or seaman under a penalty of one hundred lashes; and in addition, any member of the expedition denying it in the future was to have his tongue cut out.

No one will pretend that this was the action of a sane man; neither will any one wonder that Columbus was something less than sane after all he had gone through, and with the beginnings of a serious illness already in his blood. His achievement was slipping from his grasp; the gold had not been found, the wonders of the East had not been discovered; and it was his instinct to secure something from the general wreck that seemed to be falling about him, and to force his own dreams to come true, that caused him to cut this grim and fantastic legal caper off the coast of Cuba. He thought it at the time unlikely, seeing the difficulties of navigation that he had gone through, which he might be pardoned for regarding as insuperable to a less skilful mariner, that any one should ever come that way again; even he himself said that he would never risk his life again in such a place. He wished his journey, therefore, not to have been made in vain; and as he himself believed that he had stood on the mainland of Asia he took care to take back with him the only kind of evidence that was possible namely, the sworn affidavits of the ships' crews.

Perhaps in his madness he would really have gone on and tried to reach the Golden Chersonesus of Ptolemy, which according to Marco Polo lay just beyond, and so to steer homeward round Ceylon and the Cape of Good Hope; in which case he would either have been lost or would have discovered Mexico. The crews, however, would not hear of the voyage being continued westward. The ships were leaking and the salt water was spoiling the already doubtful provisions and he was forced to turn back. He stood to the south-east, and reached the Isle of Pines, to which he gave the name of Evangelista, where the water-casks were filled, and from there he tried to sail back to the east. But he found himself surrounded by islands and banks in every direction, which made any straight course impossible. He sailed south and east and west and north, and found himself always back again in the middle of this charmed group of islands. He spent almost a month trying to escape from them, and once his ship went ashore on a sandbank and was only warped off with the greatest difficulty. On July 7th he was back again in the region of the "Queen's Gardens," from which he stood across to the coast of Cuba.

He anchored and landed there, and being in great distress and difficulty he had a large cross erected on the mainland, and had mass said. When the Spaniards rose from their knees they saw an old native man observing them; and the old man came and sat down beside Columbus and talked to him through the interpreter. He told him that he had been in Jamaica and Espanola as well as in Cuba, and that the coming of the Spaniards had caused great distress to the people of the islands.

He then spoke to Columbus about religion, and the gist of what he said was something like this: "The performance of your worship seems good to me. You believe that this life is not everything; so do we; and I know that when this life is over there are two places reserved for me, to one of which I shall certainly go; one happy and beautiful, one dreadful and miserable. Joy and kindness reign in the one place, which is good enough for the best of men; and they will go there who while they have lived on the earth have loved peace and goodness, and who have never robbed or killed or been unkind. The other place is evil and full of shadows, and is reserved for those who disturb and hurt the sons of men; how important it is, therefore, that one should do no evil or injury in this world!"

Columbus replied with a brief statement of his own theological views, and added that he had been sent to find out if there were any persons in those islands who did evil to others, such as the Caribs or cannibals, and that if so he had come to punish them. The effect of this ingenuous speech was heightened by a gift of hawks' bells and pieces of broken glass; upon receiving which the good old man fell down on his knees, and said that the Spaniards must surely have come from heaven.

A few days later the voyage to the, south-east was resumed, and some progress was made along the coast. But contrary winds arose which made it impossible for the ships to round Cape Cruz, and Columbus decided to employ the time of waiting in completing his explorations in Jamaica. He therefore sailed due south until he once more sighted the beautiful northern coast of that island, following it to the west and landing, as his custom was, whenever he saw a good harbour or anchorage. The wind was still from the east, and he spent a month beating to the eastward along the south coast of the island, fascinated by its beauty, and willing to stay and explore it, but prevented by the discontent of his crews, who were only anxious to get back to Espanola. He had friendly interviews with many of the natives of Jamaica, and at almost the last harbour at which he touched a cacique with his wife and family and complete retinue came off in canoes to the ship, begging Columbus to take him and his household back to Spain.

Columbus considers this family, and thinks wistfully how well they would look in Barcelona. Father dressed in a cap of gold and green jewels, necklace and earrings of the same; mother decked out in similar regalia, with the addition of a small cotton apron; two sons and five brothers dressed principally in a feather or two; two daughters mother-naked, except that the elder, a handsome girl of eighteen, wears a jewelled girdle from which depends a tablet as big as an ivy leaf, made of various coloured stones embroidered on cotton. What an exhibit for one of the triumphal processions: "Native royal family, complete"! But Columbus thinks also of the scarcity of provisions on board his ships, and wonders how all these royalties would like to live on a pint of sour wine and a rotten biscuit each per day. Alas! there is not sour wine and rotten biscuit enough for his own people; it is still a long way to Espanola; and he is obliged to make polite excuses, and to say that he will come back for his majesty another time.

It was on the 20th of August that Columbus, having the day before seen the last of the dim blue hills of Jamaica, sighted again the long peninsula of Hayti, called by him Cape San Miguel, but known to us as Cape Tiburon; although it was not until he was hailed by a cacique who called out to him "Almirante, Almirante," that the seaworn mariners realised with joy that the island must be Espanola. But they were a long way from Isabella yet. They sailed along the south coast, meeting contrary winds, and at one point landing nine men who were to cross the island, and try to reach Isabella by land. Week followed week, and they made very poor progress. In the beginning of September they were caught in a severe tempest, which separated the ships for a time, and held the Admiral weather-bound for eight days. There was an eclipse of the moon during this period, and he took advantage of it to make an observation for longitude, by which he found himself to be 5 hrs. 23 min., or 80 deg. 40', west of Cadiz. In this observation there is an error of eighteen degrees, the true longitude of the island of Saona, where the observation was taken, being 62 deg. 20' west of Cadiz; and the error is accounted for partly by the inaccuracy of the tables of Regiomontanus and partly by the crudity and inexactness of the Admiral's methods. On the 24th of September they at last reached the easternmost point of Espanola, named by Columbus San Rafael. They stood to the east a little longer, and discovered the little island of Mona, which lies between Espanola and Puerto Rico; and from thence shaped their course west-by-north for Isabella. And no sooner had the course been set for home than the Admiral suddenly and completely collapsed; was carried unconscious to his cabin; and lay there in such extremity that his companions gave him up for lost.

It is no ordinary strain to which poor Christopher has succumbed. He has been five months at sea, sharing with the common sailors their bad food and weary vigils, but bearing alone on his own shoulders a weight of anxiety of which they knew nothing. Watch has relieved watch on his ships, but there has been no one to relieve him, or to lift the burden from his mind. The eyes of a nation are upon him, watchful and jealous eyes that will not forgive him any failure; and to earn their approval he has taken this voyage of five months, during which he has only been able to forget his troubles in the brief hours of slumber. Strange uncharted seas, treacherous winds and currents, drenching surges have all done their part in bringing him to this pass; and his body, now starved on rotten biscuits, now glutted with unfamiliar fruits, has been preyed upon by the tortured mind as the mind itself has been shaken and loosened by the weakness of the body. He lies there in his cabin in a deep stupor; memory, sight, and all sensation completely gone from him; dead but for the heart that beats on faintly, and the breath that comes and goes through the parted lips. Nino, de la Cosa, and the others come and look at him, shake their heads, and go away again. There is nothing to be done; perhaps they will get him back to Isabella in time to bury him there; perhaps not.

And meanwhile they are back again in calm and safe waters, and coasting a familiar shore; and the faithful little Nina, shaking out her wings in the sunny breezes, trips under the guidance of unfamiliar hands towards her moorings in the Bay of Isabella. It is a sad company that she carries; for in the cabin, deaf and blind and unconscious, there lies the heart and guiding spirit of the New World. He does not hear the talking of the waters past the Nina's timbers, does not hear the stamping on the deck and shortening of sail and unstopping of cables and getting out of gear; does not hear the splash of the anchor, nor the screams of birds that rise circling from the shore. Does not hear the greetings and the news; does not see bending over him a kind, helpful, and well-beloved face. He sees and hears and knows nothing; and in that state of rest and absence from the body they carry him, still living and breathing, ashore.

CHAPTER II

THE CONQUEST OF ESPANOLA

We must now go back to the time when Columbus, having made what arrangements he could for the safety of Espanola, left it under the charge of his brother James. Ojeda had duly marched into the interior and taken over the command of Fort St. Thomas, thus setting free Margarite, according to his instructions, to lead an expedition for purposes of reconnoitre and demonstration through the island. These, at any rate, were Margarite's orders, duly communicated to him by Ojeda; but Margarite will have none of them. Well born, well educated, well bred, he ought at least to have the spirit to carry out orders so agreeable to a gentleman of adventure; but unfortunately, although Margarite is a gentleman by birth, he is a low and dishonest dog by nature. He cannot take the decent course, cannot even play the man, and take his share in the military work of the colony. Instead of cutting paths through the forest, and exhibiting his military strength in an orderly and proper way as the Admiral intended he should, he marches forth from St. Thomas, on hearing that Columbus has sailed away, and encamps no further off than the Vega Real, that pleasant place of green valleys and groves and murmuring rivers. He encamps there, takes up his quarters there, will not budge from there for any Admiral; and as for James Columbus and his counsellors, they may go to the devil for all Margarite cares. One of them at least, he knows—Friar Buil—is not such a fool as to sit down under the command of that solemn-faced, uncouth young snip from Genoa; and doubtless when he is tired of the Vega Real he and Buil can arrange something between them. In the meantime, here is a very beautiful sunshiny place, abounding in all kinds of provisions; food for more than one kind of appetite, as he has noticed when he has thrust his rude way into the native houses and seen the shapely daughters of the islanders. He has a little army of soldiers to forage for him; they can get him food and gold, and they are useful also in those other marauding expeditions designed to replenish the seraglio that he has established in his camp; and if they like to do a little marauding and woman-stealing on their own account, it is no affair of his, and may keep the devils in a good temper. Thus Don Pedro Margarite to himself.

The peaceable and gentle natives soon began to resent these gross doings. To robbery succeeded outrage, and to outrage murder—all three committed in the very houses of the natives; and they began to murmur, to withhold that goodwill which the Spaniards had so sorely tried, and to develop a threatening attitude that was soon communicated to the natives in the vicinity of Isabella, and came under the notice of James Columbus and his council. Grave, bookish, wool-weaving young James, not used to military affairs, and not at all comfortable in his command, can think of no other expedient than—to write a letter to Margarite remonstrating with him for his licentious excesses and reminding him of the Admiral's instructions, which were being neglected.

Margarite receives the letter and reads it with a contemptuous laugh. He is not going to be ordered about by a family of Italian wool-weavers, and the only change in his conduct is that he becomes more and more careless and impudent, extending the area of his lawless operations, and making frequent visits to Isabella itself, swaggering under the very nose of solemn James, and soon deep in consultation with Friar Buil.

At this moment, that is to say very soon after the departure of Christopher on his voyage to Cuba and Jamaica, three ships dropped anchor in the Bay of Isabella. They were laden with the much-needed supplies from Spain, and had been sent out under the command of Bartholomew Columbus. It will be remembered that when Christopher reached Spain after his first voyage one of his first cares had been to write to Bartholomew, asking him to join him. The letter, doubtless after many wanderings, had found Bartholomew in France at the court of Charles VIII., by whom he was held in some esteem; in fact it was Charles who provided him with the necessary money for his journey to Spain, for Bartholomew had not greatly prospered, in spite of his voyage with Diaz to the Cape of Good Hope and of his having been in England making exploration proposals at the court of Henry VII. He had arrived in Spain after Columbus had sailed again, and had presented himself at court with his two nephews, Ferdinand and Diego, both of whom were now in the service of Prince Juan as pages. Ferdinand and Isabella seem to have received Bartholomew kindly. They liked this capable navigator, who had much of Christopher's charm of manner, and was more a man of the world than he. Much more practical also; Ferdinand would be sure to like him better than he liked Christopher, whose pompous manner and long-winded speeches bored him. Bartholomew was quick, alert, decisive and practical; he was an accomplished navigator—almost as accomplished as Columbus, as it appeared. He was offered the command of the three ships which were being prepared to go to Espanola with supplies; and he duly arrived there after a prosperous voyage. It will be remembered that Christopher had, so far as we know, kept the secret of the road to the new islands; and Bartholomew can have had nothing more to guide him than a rough chart showing the islands in a certain latitude, and the distance to be run towards them by dead-reckoning. That he should have made an exact landfall and sailed into the Bay of Isabella, never having been there before, was a certificate of the highest skill in navigation.

Unfortunately it was James who was in charge of the colony; Bartholomew had no authority, for once his ships had arrived in port his mission was accomplished until Christopher should return and find him employment. He was therefore forced to sit still and watch his young brother struggling with the unruly Spaniards. His presence, however, was no doubt a further exasperation to the malcontents. There existed in Isabella a little faction of some of the aristocrats who had never, forgiven Columbus for employing them in degrading manual labour; who had never forgiven him in fact for being there at all, and in command over them. And now here was another woolweaver, or son of a wool-weaver, come to put his finger in the pie that Christopher has apparently provided so carefully for himself and his family.

Margarite and Buil and some others, treacherous scoundrels all of them, but clannish to their own race and class, decide that they will put up with it no longer; they are tired of Espanola in any case, and Margarite, from too free indulgence among the native women, has contracted an unpleasant disease, and thinks that a sea voyage and the attentions of a Spanish doctor will be good for him. It is easy for them to put their plot into execution. There are the ships; there is nothing, for them to do but take a couple of them, provision them, and set sail for Spain, where they trust to their own influence, and the story they will be able to tell of the falseness of the Admiral's promises, to excuse their breach of discipline. And sail they do, snapping their fingers at the wool-weavers.

James and Bartholomew were perhaps glad to be rid of them, but their relief was tempered with anxiety as to the result on Christopher's reputation and favour when the malcontents should have made their false representations at Court. The brothers were powerless to do anything in that matter, however, and the state of affairs in Espanola demanded their close attention. Margarite's little army, finding itself without even the uncertain restraint of its commander, now openly mutinied and abandoned itself to the wildest excesses. It became scattered and disbanded, and little groups of soldiers went wandering about the country, robbing and outraging and carrying cruelty and oppression among the natives. Long-suffering as these were, and patiently as they bore with the unspeakable barbarities of the Spanish soldiers, there came a point beyond which their forbearance would not go. An aching spirit of unforgiveness and revenge took the place of their former gentleness and compliance; and here and there, when the Spaniards were more brutal and less cautious than was their brutal and incautious habit, the natives fell upon them and took swift and bloody revenge. Small parties found themselves besieged and put to death whole villages, whose hospitality had been abused, cut off wandering groups of the marauders and burned the houses where they lodged. The disaffection spread; and Caonabo, who had never abated his resentment at the Spanish intrusion into the island, thought the time had come to make another demonstration of native power.

Fortunately for the Spaniards his object was the fort of St. Thomas, commanded by the alert Ojeda; and this young man, who was not easily to be caught napping, had timely intelligence of his intention. When Caonabo, mustering ten thousand men, suddenly surrounded the fort and prepared to attack it, he found the fifty Spaniards of the garrison more than ready for him, and his naked savages dared not advance within the range of the crossbows and arquebuses. Caonabo tried to besiege the station, watching every gorge and road through which supplies could reach it, but Ojeda made sallies and raids upon the native force, under which it became thinned and discouraged; and Caonabo had finally to withdraw to his own territory.

But he was not yet beaten. He decided upon another and much larger enterprise, which was to induce the other caciques of the island to co-operate with him in an attack upon Isabella, the population of which he knew would have been much thinned and weakened by disease. The island was divided into five native provinces. The northeastern part, named Marien, was under the rule of Guacanagari, whose headquarters were near the abandoned La Navidad. The remaining eastern part of the island, called Higuay, was under a chief named Cotabanama. The western province was Xaragua, governed by one Behechio, whose sister, Anacaona, was the wife of Caonabo. The middle of the island was divided into two provinces-that which extended from the northern coast to the Cibao mountains and included the Vega Real being governed by Guarionex, and that which extended from the Cibao mountains to the south being governed by Caonabo. All these rulers were more or less embittered by the outrages and cruelties of the Spaniards, and all agreed to join with Caonabo except Guacanagari. That loyal soul, so faithful to what he knew of good, shocked and distressed as he was by outrages from which his own people had suffered no less than the others, could not bring himself to commit what he regarded as a breach of the laws of hospitality. It was upon his shores that Columbus had first landed; and although it was his own country and his own people whose wrongs were to be avenged, he could not bring himself to turn traitor to the grave Admiral with whom, in those happy days of the past, he had enjoyed so much pleasant intercourse. His refusal to co-operate delayed the plan of Caonabo, who directed the island coalition against Guacanagari himself in order to bring him to reason. He was attacked by the neighbouring chiefs; one of his wives was killed and another captured; but still he would not swerve from his ideal of conduct.

The first thing that Columbus recognised when he opened his eyes after his long period of lethargy and insensibility was the face of his brother Bartholomew bend-over him where he lay in bed in his own house at Espanola. Nothing could have been more welcome to him, sick, lonely and discouraged as he was, than the presence of that strong, helpful brother; and from the time when Bartholomew's friendly face first greeted him he began to get better. His first act, as soon as he was strong enough to sign a paper, was to appoint Bartholomew to the office of Adelantado, or Lieutenant-Governor—an indiscreet and rather tactless proceeding which, although it was not outside his power as a bearer of the royal seal, was afterwards resented by King Ferdinand as a piece of impudent encroachment upon the royal prerogative. But Columbus was unable to transact business himself, and James was manifestly of little use; the action was natural enough.

In the early days of his convalescence he had another pleasant experience, in the shape of a visit from Guacanagari, who came to express his concern at the Admiral's illness, and to tell him the story of what had been going on in his absence. The gentle creature referred again with tears to the massacre at La Navidad, and again asserted that innocence of any hand in it which Columbus had happily never doubted; and he told him also of the secret league against Isabella, of his own refusal to join it, and of the attacks to which he had consequently been subjected. It must have been an affecting meeting for these two, who represented the first friendship formed between the Old World and the New, who were both of them destined to suffer in the impact of civilisation and savagery, and whose names and characters were happily destined to survive that impact, and to triumph over the oblivion of centuries.

So long as the native population remained hostile and unconquered by kindness or force, it was impossible to work securely at the development of the colony; and Columbus, however regretfully, had come to feel that circumstances more or less obliged him to use force. At first he did not quite realise the gravity of the position, and attempted to conquer or reconcile the natives in little groups. Guarionex, the cacique of the Vega Real, was by gifts and smooth words soothed back into a friendship which was consolidated by the marriage of his daughter with Columbus's native interpreter. It was useless, how ever, to try and make friends with Caonabo, that fierce irreconcilable; and it was felt that only by stratagem could he be secured. No sooner was this suggested than Ojeda volunteered for the service. Amid the somewhat slow-moving figures of our story this man appears as lively as a flea; and he dances across our pages in a sensation of intrepid feats of arms that make his great popularity among the Spaniards easily credible to us. He did not know what fear was; he was always ready for a fight of any kind; a quarrel in the streets of Madrid, a duel, a fight with a man or a wild beast, a brawl in a tavern or a military expedition, were all the same to him, if only they gave him an opportunity for fighting. He had a little picture of the Virgin hung round his neck, by which he swore, and to which he prayed; he had never been so much as scratched in all his affrays, and he believed that he led a charmed life. Who would go out against Caonabo, the Goliath of the island? He, little David Ojeda, he would go out and undertake to fetch the giant back with him; and all he wanted was ten men, a pair of handcuffs, a handful of trinkets, horses for the whole of his company, and his little image or picture of the Virgin.

Columbus may have smiled at this proposal, but he knew his man; and Ojeda duly departed with his horses and his ten men. Plunging into the forest, he made his way through sixty leagues of dense undergrowth until he arrived in the very heart of Caonabo's territory and presented himself at the chiefs house. The chief was at home, and, not unimpressed by the valour of Ojeda, who represented himself as coming on a friendly mission, received him under conditions of truce. He had an eye for military prowess, this Caonabo, and something of the lion's heart in him; he recognised in Ojeda the little man who kept him so long at bay outside Fort St. Thomas; and, after the manner of lion-hearted people, liked him none the worse for that.

Ojeda proposes that the King should accompany him to Isabella to make peace. No, says Caonabo. Then Ojeda tries another way. There is a poetical side to this big fighting savage, and often in more friendly days, when the bell in the little chapel of Isabella has been ringing for Vespers, the cacique has been observed sitting alone on some hill listening, enchanted by the strange silver voice that floated to him across the sunset. The bell has indeed become something of a personality in the island: all the neighbouring savages listen to its voice with awe and fascination, pausing with inclined heads whenever it begins to speak from its turret.

Ojeda talks to Caonabo about the bell, and tells him what a wonderful thing it is; tells him also that if he will come with him to Isabella he shall have the bell for a present. Poetry and public policy struggle together in Caonabo's heart, but poetry wins; the great powerful savage, urged thereto by his childish lion-heart, will come to Isabella if they will give him the bell. He sets forth, accompanied by a native retinue, and by Ojeda and his ten horsemen. Presently they come to a river and Ojeda produces his bright manacles; tells the King that they are royal ornaments and that he has been instructed to bestow them upon Caonabo as a sign of honour. But first he must come alone to the river and bathe, which he does. Then he must sit with Ojeda upon his horse; which he does. Then he must have fitted on to him the shining silver trinkets; which he does, the great grinning giant, pleased with his toys. Then, to show him what it is like to be on a horse, Ojeda canters gently round in widening and ever widening circles; a turn of his spurred heels, and the canter becomes a gallop, the circle becomes a straight line, and Caonabo is on the road to Isabella. When they are well beyond reach of the natives they pause and tie Caonabo securely into his place; and by this treachery bring him into Isabella, where he is imprisoned in the Admiral's house.

The sulky giant, brought thus into captivity, refuses to bend his proud, stubborn heart into even a form of submission. He takes no notice of Columbus, and pays him no honour, although honour is paid to himself as a captive king. He sits there behind his bars gnawing his fingers, listening to the voice of the bell that has lured him into captivity, and thinking of the free open life which he is to know no more. Though he will pay no deference to the Admiral, will not even rise when he enters his presence, there is one person he holds in honour, and that is Ojeda. He will not rise when the Admiral comes; but when Ojeda comes, small as he is, and without external state, the chief makes his obeisance to him. The Admiral he sets at defiance, and boasts of his destruction of La Navidad, and of his plan to destroy Isabella; Ojeda he respects and holds in honour, as being the only man in the island brave enough to come into his house and carry him off a captive. There is a good deal of the sportsman in Caonabo.

The immediate result of the capture of Caonabo was to rouse the islanders to further hostilities, and one of the brothers of the captive king led a force of seven thousand men to the vicinity of St. Thomas, to which Ojeda, however, had in the meantime returned. His small force was augmented by some men despatched by Bartholomew Columbus on receipt of an urgent message; and in command of this force Ojeda sallied forth against the natives and attacked them furiously on horse and on foot, killing a great part of them, taking others prisoner, and putting the rest to flight. This was the beginning of the end of the island resistance. A month or two later, when Columbus was better, he and Bartholomew together mustered the whole of their available army and marched out in search of the native force, which he knew had been rallied and greatly augmented.

The two forces met near the present town of Santiago, in the plain known as the Savanna of Matanza. The Spanish force was divided into three main divisions, under the command of Christopher and Bartholomew Columbus and Ojeda respectively. These three divisions attacked the Indians simultaneously from different points, Ojeda throwing his cavalry upon them, riding them down, and cutting them to pieces. Drums were beaten and trumpets blown; the guns were fired from the cover of the trees; and a pack of bloodhounds, which had been sent out from Spain with

Bartholomew, were let loose upon the natives and tore their bodies to pieces. It was an easy and horrible victory. The native force was estimated by Columbus at one hundred thousand men, although we shall probably be nearer the mark if we reduce that estimate by one half.

The powers of hell were let loose that day into the Earthly Paradise. The guns mowed red lines of blood through the solid ranks of the natives; the great Spanish horses trod upon and crushed their writhing bodies, in which arrows and lances continually stuck and quivered; and the ferocious dogs, barking and growling, seized the naked Indians by the throat, dragged them to the ground, and tore out their very entrails . . . . Well for us that the horrible noises of that day are silent now; well for the world that that place of bloodshed and horror has grown green again; better for us and for the world if those cries had never been heard, and that quiet place had never received a stain that centuries of green succeeding springtides can never wash away.

It was some time before this final battle that the convalescence of the Admiral was further assisted by the arrival of four ships commanded by Antonio Torres, who must have passed, out of sight and somewhere on the high seas, the ships bearing Buil and Margarite back to Spain. He brought with him a large supply of fresh provisions for the colony, and a number of genuine colonists, such as fishermen, carpenters, farmers, mechanics, and millers. And better still he brought a letter from the Sovereigns, dated the 16th of August 1494, which did much to cheer the shaken spirits of Columbus. The words with which he had freighted his empty ships had not been in vain; and in this reply to them he was warmly commended for his diligence, and reminded that he enjoyed the unshaken confidence of the Sovereigns. They proposed that a caravel should sail every month from Spain and from Isabella, bearing intelligence of the colony and also, it was hoped, some of its products. In a general letter addressed to the colony the settlers were reminded of the obedience they owed to the Admiral, and were instructed to obey him in all things under the penalty of heavy fines. They invited Columbus to come back if he could in order to be present at the convention which was to establish the line of demarcation between Spanish and Portuguese possessions; or if he could not come himself to send his brother Bartholomew. There were reasons, however, which made this difficult. Columbus wished to despatch the ships back again as speedily as possible, in order that news of him might help to counteract the evil rumours that he knew Buil and Margarite would be spreading. He himself was as yet (February 1494) too ill to travel; and during his illness Bartholomew could not easily be spared. It was therefore decided to send home James, who could most easily be spared, and whose testimony as a member of the governing body during the absence of the Admiral on his voyage to Cuba might be relied upon to counteract the jealous accusations of Margarite and Buil.

Unfortunately there was no golden cargo to send back with him. As much gold as possible was scraped together, but it was very little. The usual assortment of samples of various island products was also sent; but still the vessels were practically empty. Columbus must have been painfully conscious that the time for sending samples had more than expired, and that the people in Spain might reasonably expect some of the actual riches of which there had been so many specimens and promises. In something approaching desperation, he decided to fill the empty holds of the ships with something which, if it was not actual money, could at least be made to realise money. From their sunny dreaming life on the island five hundred natives were taken and lodged in the dark holds of the caravels, to be sent to Spain and sold there for what they would fetch. Of course they were to be "freed" and converted to Christianity in the process; that was always part of the programme, but it did not interfere with business. They were not man-eating Caribs or fierce marauding savages from neighbouring islands, but were of the mild and peaceable race that peopled Espanola. The wheels of civilisation were beginning to turn in the New World.

After the capture of Caonabo and the massacre of April 25th Columbus marched through the island, receiving the surrender and submission of the terrified natives. At the approach of his force the caciques came out and sued for peace; and if here and there there was a momentary resistance, a charge of cavalry soon put an end to it. One by one the kings surrendered and laid down their arms, until all the island rulers had capitulated with the exception of Behechio, into whose territory Columbus did not march, and who sullenly retired to the south-western corner of the island. The terms of peace were harsh enough, and were suggested by the dilemma of Columbus in his frantic desire to get together some gold at any cost. A tribute of gold-dust was laid upon every adult native in the island. Every three months a hawk's bell full of gold was to be brought to the treasury at Isabella, and in the case 39 of caciques the measure was a calabash. A receipt in the form of a brass medal was fastened to the neck of every Indian when he paid his tribute, and those who could not show the medal with the necessary number of marks were to be further fined and punished. In the districts where there was no gold, 25 lbs. of cotton was accepted instead.

This levy was made in ignorance of the real conditions under which the natives possessed themselves of the gold. What they had in many cases represented the store of years, and in all but one or two favoured districts it was quite impossible for them to keep up the amount of the tribute. Yet the hawks' bells, which once had been so eagerly coveted and were now becoming hated symbols of oppression, had to be filled somehow; and as the day of payment drew near the wretched natives, who had formerly only sought for gold when a little of it was wanted for a pretty ornament, had now to work with frantic energy in the river sands; or in other cases, to toil through the heat of the day in the cotton fields which they had formerly only cultivated enough to furnish their very scant requirements of use and adornment. One or two caciques, knowing that their people could not possibly furnish the required amount of gold, begged that its value in grain might be accepted instead; but that was not the kind of wealth that Columbus was seeking. It must be gold or nothing; and rather than receive any other article from the gold-bearing districts, he consented to take half the amount.

Thus step by step, and under the banner of the Holy Catholic religion, did dark and cruel misery march through the groves and glades of the island and banish for ever its ancient peace. This long-vanished race that was native to the island of Espanola seems to have had some of the happiest and most lovable qualities known to dwellers on this planet. They had none of the brutalities of the African, the paralysing wisdom of the Asian, nor the tragic potentialities of the European peoples. Their life was from day to day, and from season to season, like the life of flowers and birds. They lived in such order and peaceable community as the common sense of their own simple needs suggested; they craved no pleasures except those that came free from nature, and sought no wealth but what the sun gave them. In their verdant island, near to the heart and source of light, surrounded by the murmur of the sea, and so enriched by nature that the idea, of any other kind of riches never occurred to them, their existence went to a happy dancing measure like that of the fauns and nymphs in whose charmed existence they believed. The sun and moon were to them creatures of their island who had escaped from a cavern by the shore and now wandered free in the upper air, peopling it with happy stars; and man himself they believed to have sprung from crevices in the rocks, like the plants that grew tall and beautiful wherever there was a handful of soil for their roots. Poor happy children! You are all dead a long while ago now, and have long been hushed in the great humming sleep and silence of Time; the modern world has no time nor room for people like you, with so much kindness and so little ambition . . . . Yet their free pagan souls were given a chance to be penned within the Christian fold; the priest accompanied the gunner and the bloodhound, the missionary walked beside the slave-driver; and upon the bewildered sun-bright surface of their minds the shadow of the cross was for a moment thrown. Verily to them the professors of Christ brought not peace, but a sword.

CHAPTER III

UPS AND DOWNS

While Columbus was toiling under the tropical sun to make good his promises to the Crown, Margarite and Buil, having safely come home to Spain from across the seas, were busy setting forth their view of the value of his discoveries. It was a view entirely different from any that Ferdinand and Isabella had heard before, and coming as it did from two men of position and importance who had actually been in Espanola, and were loyal and religious subjects of the Crown, it could not fail to receive, if not immediate and complete credence, at any rate grave attention. Hitherto the Sovereigns had only heard one side of the matter; an occasional jealous voice may have been raised from the neighbourhood of the Pinzons or some one else not entirely satisfied with his own position in the affair; but such small cries of dissent had naturally had little chance against the dignified eloquence of the Admiral.

Now, however, the matter was different. People who were at least the equals of Columbus in intelligence, and his superiors by birth and education, had seen with their own eyes the things of which he had spoken, and their account differed widely from his. They represented things in Espanola as being in a very bad way indeed, which was true enough; drew a dismal picture of an overcrowded colony ravaged with disease and suffering from lack of provisions; and held forth at length upon the very doubtful quality of the gold with which the New World was supposed to abound. More than this, they brought grave charges against Columbus himself, representing him as unfit to govern a colony, given to favouritism, and, worst of all, guilty of having deliberately misrepresented for his own ends the resources of the colony. This as we know was not true. It was not for his own ends, or for any ends at all within the comprehension of men like Margarite and Buil, that poor Christopher had spoken so glowingly out of a heart full of faith in what he had seen and done. Purposes, dim perhaps, but far greater and loftier than any of which these two mean souls had understanding, animated him alike in his discoveries and in his account of them; although that does not alter the unpleasant fact that at the stage matters had now reached it seemed as though there might have been serious misrepresentation.

Ferdinand and Isabella, thus confronted with a rather difficult situation, acted with great wisdom and good sense. How much or how little they believed we do not know, but it was obviously their duty, having heard such an account from responsible officers, to investigate matters for themselves without assuming either that the report was true or untrue. They immediately had four caravels furnished with supplies, and decided to appoint an agent to accompany the expedition, investigate the affairs of the colony, and make a report to them. If the Admiral was still absent when their agent reached the colony he was to be entrusted with the distribution of the supplies which were being sent out; for Columbus's long absence from Espanola had given rise to some fears for his safety.

The Sovereigns had just come to this decision (April 1495) when a letter arrived from the Admiral himself, announcing his return to Espanola after discovering the veritable mainland of Asia, as the notarial document enclosed with the letter attested. Torres and James Columbus had arrived in Spain, bearing the memorandum which some time ago we saw the Admiral writing; and they were able to do something towards allaying the fears of the Sovereigns as to the condition of the colony. The King and Queen, nevertheless, wisely decided to carry out their original intention, and in appointing an agent they very handsomely chose one of the men whom Columbus had recommended to them in his letter—Juan Aguado. This action shows a friendliness to Columbus and confidence in him that lead one to suspect that the tales of Margarite and Buil had been taken with a grain of salt.

At the same time the Sovereigns made one or two orders which could not but be unwelcome to Columbus. A decree was issued making it lawful for all native-born Spaniards to make voyages of discovery, and to settle in Espanola itself if they liked. This was an infringement of the original privileges granted to the Admiral— privileges which were really absurd, and which can only have been granted in complete disbelief that anything much would come of his discovery. It took Columbus two years to get this order modified, and in the meantime a great many Spanish adventurers, our old friends the Pinzons among them, did actually make voyages and added to the area explored by the Spaniards in Columbus's lifetime. Columbus was bitterly jealous that any one should be admitted to the western ocean, which he regarded as his special preserve, except under his supreme authority; and he is reported to have said that once the way to the West had been pointed out "even the very tailors turned explorers." There, surely, spoke the long dormant woolweaver in him.

The commission given to Aguado was very brief, and so vaguely worded that it might mean much or little, according to the discretion of the commissioner and the necessities of the case as viewed by him. "We send to you Juan Aguada, our Groom of the Chambers, who will speak to you on our part. We command you to give him faith and credit." A letter was also sent to Columbus in which he was instructed to reduce the number of people dependent on the colony to five hundred instead of a thousand; and the control of the mines was entrusted to one Pablo Belvis, who was sent out as chief metallurgist. As for the slaves that Columbus had sent home, Isabella forbade their sale until inquiry could be made into the condition of their capture, and the fine moral point involved was entrusted to the ecclesiastical authorities for examination and solution. Poor Christopher, knowing as he did that five hundred heretics were being burned every year by the Grand Inquisitor, had not expected this hair-splitting over the fate of heathens who had rebelled against Spanish authority; and it caused him some distress when he heard of it. The theologians, however, proved equal to the occasion, and the slaves were duly sold in Seville market.

Aguado sailed from Cadiz at the end of August 1495, and reached Espanola in October. James Columbus (who does not as yet seem to be in very great demand anywhere, and who doubtless conceals behind his grave visage much honest amazement at the amount of life that he is seeing) returned with him. Aguado, on arriving at Isabella, found that Columbus was absent establishing forts in the interior of the island, Bartholomew being left in charge at Isabella.

Aguado, who had apparently been found faithful in small matters, was found wanting in his use of the authority that had been entrusted to him. It seems to have turned his head; for instead of beginning quietly to investigate the affairs of the colony as he had been commanded to do he took over from Bartholomew the actual government, and interpreted his commission as giving him the right to supersede the Admiral himself. The unhappy colony, which had no doubt been enjoying some brief period of peace under the wise direction of Bartholomew, was again thrown into confusion by the doings of Aguado. He arrested this person, imprisoned that; ordered that things should be done this way, which had formerly been done that way; and if they had formerly been done that way, then he ordered that they should be done this way—in short he committed every mistake possible for a man in his situation armed with a little brief authority. He did not hesitate to let it be known that he was there to examine the conduct of the Admiral himself; and we may be quite sure that every one in the colony who had a grievance or an ill tale to carry, carried it to Aguado. His whole attitude was one of enmity and disloyalty to the Admiral who had so handsomely recommended him to the notice of the Sovereigns; and so undisguised was his attitude that even the Indians began to lodge their complaints and to see a chance by which they might escape from the intolerable burden of the gold tribute.

It was at this point that Columbus returned and found Aguado ruling in the place of Bartholomew, who had wisely made no protest against his own deposition, but was quietly waiting for the Admiral to return. Columbus might surely have been forgiven if he had betrayed extreme anger and annoyance at the doings of Aguado; and it is entirely to his credit that he concealed such natural wrath as he may have felt, and greeted Aguado with extreme courtesy and ceremony as a representative of the Sovereigns. He made no protest, but decided to return himself to Spain and confront the jealousy and ill-fame that were accumulating against him.

Just as the ships were all ready to sail, one of the hurricanes which occur periodically in the West Indies burst upon the island, lashing the sea into a wall of advancing foam that destroyed everything before it. Among other things it destroyed three out of the four ships, dashing them on the beach and reducing them to complete wreckage. The only one that held to her anchor and, although much battered and damaged, rode out the gale, was the Nina, that staunch little friend that had remained faithful to the Admiral through so many dangers and trials. There was nothing for it but to build a new ship out of the fragments of the wrecks, and to make the journey home with two ships instead of with four.

At this moment, while he was waiting for the ship to be completed, Columbus heard a piece of news of a kind that never failed to rouse his interest. There was a young Spaniard named Miguel Diaz who had got into disgrace in Isabella some time before on account of a duel, and had wandered into the island until he had come out on the south coast at the mouth of the river Ozama, near the site of the present town of Santo Domingo. There he had fallen in love with a female cacique and had made his home with her. She, knowing the Spanish taste, and anxious to please her lover and to retain him in her territory, told him of some rich gold-mines that there were in the neighbourhood, and suggested that he should inform the Admiral, who would perhaps remove the settlement from Isabella to the south coast. She provided him with guides and sent him off to Isabella, where, hearing that his antagonist had recovered, and that he himself was therefore in no danger of punishment, he presented himself with his story.

Columbus immediately despatched Bartholomew with a party to examine the mines; and sure enough they found in the river Hayna undoubted evidence of a wealth far in excess of that contained in the Cibao gold-mines. Moreover, they had noticed two ancient excavations about which the natives could tell them nothing, but which made them think that the mines had once been worked.

Columbus was never backward in fitting a story and a theory to whatever phenomena surrounded him; and in this case he was certain that the excavations were the work of

Solomon, and that he had discovered the gold of Ophir. "Sure enough," thinks the Admiral, "I have hit it this time; and the ships came eastward from the Persian Gulf round the Golden Chersonesus, which I discovered this very last winter." Immediately, as his habit was, Columbus began to build castles in Spain. Here was a fine answer to Buil and Margarite! Without waiting a week or two to get any of the gold this extraordinary man decided to hurry off at once to Spain with the news, not dreaming that Spain might, by this time, have had a surfeit of news, and might be in serious need of some simple, honest facts. But he thought his two caravels sufficiently freighted with this new belief—the belief that he had discovered the Ophir of Solomon.

The Admiral sailed on March 10th, 1496, carrying with him in chains the vanquished Caonabo and other natives. He touched at Marigalante and at Guadaloupe, where his people had an engagement with the natives, taking several prisoners, but releasing them all again with the exception of one woman, a handsome creature who had fallen in love with Caonabo and refused to go. But for Caonabo the joys of life and love were at an end; his heart and spirit were broken. He was not destined to be paraded as a captive through the streets of Spain, and it was somewhere in the deep Atlantic that he paid the last tribute to the power that had captured and broken him. He died on the voyage, which was longer and much more full of hardships than usual. For some reason or other Columbus did not take the northerly route going home, but sailed east from Gaudaloupe, encountering the easterly trade winds, which delayed him so much that the voyage occupied three months instead of six weeks.

Once more he exhibited his easy mastery of the art of navigation and his extraordinary gift for estimating dead-reckoning. After having been out of sight of land for eight weeks, and while some of the sailors thought they might be in the Bay of Biscay, and others that they were in the English Channel, the Admiral suddenly announced that they were close to Cape Saint Vincent.

No land was in sight, but he ordered that sail should be shortened that evening; and sure enough the next morning they sighted the land close by Cape Saint Vincent. Columbus managed his landfalls with a fine dramatic sense as though they were conjuring tricks; and indeed they must have seemed like conjuring tricks, except that they were almost always successful.

CHAPTER IV

IN SPAIN AGAIN

The loiterers about the harbour of Cadiz saw a curious sight on June 11th, 1496, when the two battered ships, bearing back the voyagers from the Eldorado of the West, disembarked their passengers. There were some 220 souls on board, including thirty Indians: and instead of leaping ashore, flushed with health, and bringing the fortunes which they had gone out to seek, they crawled miserably from the boats or were carried ashore, emaciated by starvation, yellow with disease, ragged and unkempt from poverty, and with practically no possessions other than the clothes they stood up in. Even the Admiral, now in his forty-sixth year, hardly had the appearance that one would expect in a Viceroy of the Indies. His white hair and beard were rough and matted, his handsome face furrowed by care and sunken by illness and exhaustion, and instead of the glittering armour and uniform of his office he wore the plain robe and girdle of the Franciscan order—this last probably in consequence of some vow or other he had made in an hour of peril on the voyage.

One lucky coincidence marked his arrival. In the harbour, preparing to weigh anchor, was a fleet of three little caravels, commanded by Pedro Nino, about to set out for Espanola with supplies and despatches. Columbus hurried on board Nino's ship, and there read the letters from the Sovereigns which it had been designed he should receive in Espanola. The letters are not preserved, but one can make a fair guess at their contents. Some searching questions would certainly be asked, kind assurances of continued confidence would doubtless be given, with many suggestions for the betterment of affairs in the distant colony. Only their result upon the Admiral is known to us. He sat down there and then and wrote to Bartholomew, urging him to secure peace in the island by every means in his power, to send home any caciques or natives who were likely to give trouble, and most of all to push on with the building of a settlement on the south coast where the new mines were, and to have a cargo of gold ready to send back with the next expedition. Having written this letter, the Admiral saw the little fleet sail away on June 17th, and himself prepared with mingled feelings to present himself before his Sovereigns.

While he was waiting for their summons at Los Palacios, a small town near Seville, he was the guest of the curate of that place, Andrez Bernaldez, who had been chaplain to Christopher's old friend DEA, the Archbishop of Seville. This good priest evidently proved a staunch friend to Columbus at this anxious period of his life, for the Admiral left many important papers in his charge when he again left Spain, and no small part of the scant contemporary information about Columbus that has come down to us is contained in the 'Historia de los Reyes Catolicos', which Bernaldez wrote after the death of Columbus.

Fickle Spain had already forgotten its first sentimental enthusiasm over the Admiral's discoveries, and now was only interested in their financial results. People cannot be continually excited about a thing which they have not seen, and there were events much nearer home that absorbed the public interest. There was the trouble with France, the contemplated alliance of the Crown Prince with Margaret of Austria, and of the Spanish Princess Juana with Philip of Austria; and there were the designs of Ferdinand upon the kingdom of Naples, which was in his eyes a much more desirable and valuable prize than any group of unknown islands beyond the ocean.

Columbus did his very best to work up enthusiasm again. He repeated the performance that had been such a success after his first voyage—the kind of circus procession in which the natives were marched in column surrounded by specimens of the wealth of the Indies. But somehow it did not work so well this time. Where there had formerly been acclamations and crowds pressing forward to view the savages and their ornaments, there were now apathy and a dearth of spectators. And although Columbus did his very best, and was careful to exhibit every scrap of gold that he had brought, and to hang golden collars and ornaments about the necks of the marching Indians, his exhibition was received either in ominous silence or, in some quarters, with something like derision. As I have said before, there comes a time when the best-disposed debtors do not regard themselves as being repaid by promises, and when the most enthusiastic optimist desires to see something more than samples. It was only old Colon going round with his show again—flamingoes, macaws, seashells, dye-woods, gums and spices; some people laughed, and some were angry; but all were united in thinking that the New World was not a very profitable speculation.

Things were a little better, however, at Court. Isabella certainly believed still in Columbus; Ferdinand, although he had never been enthusiastic, knew the Admiral too well to make the vulgar mistake of believing him an impostor; and both were too polite and considerate to add to his obvious mortification and distress by any discouraging comments. Moreover, the man himself had lost neither his belief in the value of his discoveries nor his eloquence in talking of them; and when he told his story to the Sovereigns they could not help being impressed, not only with his sincerity but with his ability and single-heartedness also. It was almost the same old story, of illimitable wealth that was just about to be acquired, and perhaps no one but

Columbus could have made it go down once more with success; but talking about his exploits was never any trouble to him, and his astonishing conviction, the lofty and dignified manner in which he described both good and bad fortune, and the impressive way in which he spoke of the wealth of the gold of Ophir and of the far-reaching importance of his supposed discovery of the Golden Chersonesus and the mainland of Asia, had their due effect on his hearers.

It was always his way, plausible Christopher, to pass lightly over the premises and to dwell with elaborate detail on the deductions. It was by no means proved that he had discovered the mines of King Solomon; he had never even seen the place which he identified with them; it was in fact nothing more than an idea in his own head; but we may be sure that he took it as an established fact that he had actually discovered the mines of Ophir, and confined his discussion to estimates of the wealth which they were likely to yield, and of what was to be done with the wealth when the mere details of conveying it from the mines to the ships had been disposed of. So also with the Golden Chersonesus. The very name was enough to stop the mouths of doubters; and here was the man himself who had actually been there, and here was a sworn affidavit from every member of his crew to say that they had been there too. This kind of logic is irresistible if you only grant the first little step; and Columbus had the art of making it seem an act of imbecility in any of his hearers to doubt the strength of the little link by which his great golden chains of argument were fastened to fact and truth.

For Columbus everything depended upon his reception by the Sovereigns at this time. Unless he could re-establish his hold upon them and move to a still more secure position in their confidence he was a ruined man and his career was finished; and one cannot but sympathise with him as he sits there searching his mind for tempting and convincing arguments, and speaking so calmly and gravely and confidently in spite of all the doubts and flutterings in his heart. Like a tradesman setting out his wares, he brought forth every inducement he could think of to convince the Sovereigns that the only way to make a success of what they had already done was to do more; that the only way to make profitable the money that had already been spent was to spend more; that the only way to prove the wisdom of their trust in him was to trust him more. One of his transcendent merits in a situation of this kind was that he always had something new and interesting to propose. He did not spread out his hands and say, "This is what I have done: it is the best I can do; how are you going to treat me?" He said in effect, "This is what I have done; you will see that it will all come right in time; do not worry about it; but meanwhile I have something else to propose which I think your Majesties will consider a good plan."

His new demand was for a fleet of six ships, two of which were to convey supplies to Espanola, and the other four to be entrusted to him for the purpose of a voyage of discovery towards the mainland to the south of Espanola, of which he had heard consistent rumours; which was said to be rich in gold, and (a clever touch) to which the King of Portugal was thinking of sending a fleet, as he thought that it might lie within the limits of his domain of heathendom. And so well did he manage, and so deeply did he impress the Sovereigns with his assurance that this time the thing amounted to what is vulgarly called "a dead certainty," that they promised him he should have his ships.

But promise and performance, as no one knew better than Columbus, are different things; and it was a long while before he got his ships. There was the usual scarcity of money, and the extensive military and diplomatic operations in which the Crown was then engaged absorbed every maravedi that Ferdinand could lay his hands on. There was an army to be maintained under the Pyrenees to keep watch over France; fleets had to be kept patrolling both the Mediterranean and Atlantic seaboards; and there was a whole armada required to convey the princesses of Spain and Austria to their respective husbands in connection with the double matrimonial alliance arranged between the two countries. And when at last, in October 1496, six million maravedis were provided wherewith Columbus might equip his fleet, they were withdrawn again under very mortifying circumstances. The appropriation had just been made when a letter arrived from Pedro Nino, who had been to Espanola and come back again, and now wrote from Cadiz to the Sovereigns, saying that his ships were full of gold. He did not present himself at Court, but went to visit his family at Huelva; but the good news of his letter was accepted as an excuse for this oversight.

No one was better pleased than the Admiral. "What did I tell you?" he says; "you see the mines of Hayna are paying already." King Ferdinand, equally pleased, and having an urgent need of money in connection with his operations against France, took the opportunity to cancel the appropriation of the six million maravedis, giving Columbus instead an order for the amount to be paid out of the treasure brought home by Nino. Alas, the mariner's boast of gold had been a figure of speech. There was no gold; there was only a cargo of slaves, which Nino deemed the equivalent of gold; and when Bartholomew's despatches came to be read he described the affairs of Espanola as being in very much the same condition as before. This incident produced a most unfortunate impression. Even Columbus was obliged to keep quiet for a little while; and it is likely that the mention of six million maravedis was not welcomed by him for some time afterwards.

After the wedding of Prince Juan in March 1497, when Queen Isabella had more time to give to external affairs, the promise to Columbus was again remembered, and his position was considered in detail. An order was made (April 23rd, 1497), restoring to the Admiral the original privileges bestowed upon him at Santa Fe. He was offered a large tract of land in Espanola, with the title of Duke; but much as he hankered after titular honours, he was for once prudent enough to refuse this gift. His reason was that it would only further damage his influence, and give apparent justification to those enemies who said that the whole enterprise had been undertaken merely in his own interests; and it is possible also that his many painful associations with Espanola, and the bloodshed and horrors that he had witnessed there, had aroused in his superstitious mind a distaste for possessions and titles in that devastated Paradise. Instead, he accepted a measure of relief from the obligations incurred by his eighth share in the many unprofitable expeditions that had been sent out during the last three years, agreeing for the next three years to receive an eighth share of the gross income, and a tenth of the net profits, without contributing anything to the cost. His appointment of Bartholomew to the office of Adelantado, which had annoyed Ferdinand, was now confirmed; the universal license which had been granted to Spanish subjects to settle in the new lands was revoked in so far as it infringed the Admiral's privileges; and he was granted a force of 330 officers, soldiers, and artificers to be at his personal disposal in the prosecution of his next voyage.

The death of Prince Juan in October 1497 once more distracted the attention of the Court from all but personal matters; and Columbus employed the time of waiting in drafting a testamentary document in which he was permitted to create an entail on his title and estates in favour of his two sons and their heirs for ever. This did not represent his complete or final testament, for he added codicils at various times, the latest being executed the day before his death. The document is worth studying; it reveals something of the laborious, painstaking mind reaching out down the rivers and streams of the future that were to flow from the fountain of his own greatness; it reveals also his triple conception of the obligations of human life in this world—the cultivation and retention of temporal dignity, the performance of pious and charitable acts, and the recognition of duty to one's family. It was in this document that Columbus formulated the curious cipher which he always now used in signing his name, and of which various readings are given in the Appendix. He also enjoined upon his heir the duty of using the simple title which he himself loved and used most—"The Admiral."

After the death of Prince Juan, Queen Isabella honoured Columbus by attaching his two sons to her own person as pages; and her friendship must at this time have gone far to compensate him for the coolness shown towards him by the public at large. He might talk as much as he pleased, but he had nothing to show for all his talk except a few trinkets, a collection of interesting but valueless botanical specimens, and a handful of miserable slaves. Lives and fortunes had been wrecked on the enterprise, which had so far brought nothing to Spain but the promise of luxurious adventure that was not fulfilled and of a wealth and glory that had not been realised. It must have been a very humiliating circumstance to Columbus that in the preparations which he was now (February 1498) making for the equipment of his new expedition a great difficulty was found in procuring ships and men. Not even before the first voyage had so much reluctance been shown to risk life and property in the enterprise. Merchants and sailors had then been frightened of dangers which they did not know; now, it seemed, the evils of which they did know proved a still greater deterrent. The Admiral was at this time the guest of his friend Bernaldez, who has told us something of his difficulties; and the humiliating expedient of seizing ships under a royal order had finally to be adopted. But it would never have done to impress the colonists also; that would have been too open a confession of failure for the proud Admiral to tolerate.

Instead he had recourse to the miserable plan of which he had made use in Palos; the prisons were opened, and criminals under sentence invited to come forth and enjoy the blessings of colonial life. Even then there was not that rush from the prison doors that might have been expected, and some desperate characters apparently preferred the mercies of a Spanish prison to what they had heard of the joys of the Earthly Paradise. Still a number of criminals did doubtfully crawl forth and furnish a retinue for the great Admiral and Viceroy. Trembling, suspicious, and with more than half a mind to go back to their bonds, some part of the human vermin of Spain was eventually cajoled and chivied on board the ships.

The needs of the colony being urgent, and recruiting being slow, two caravels laden with provisions were sent off in advance; but even for this purpose there was a difficulty about money, and good Isabella furnished the expense, at much inconvenience, from her private purse.

Columbus had to supervise everything himself; and no wonder that by the end of May, when he was ready to sail, his patience and temper were exhausted and his much-tried endurance broke down under the petty gnatlike irritations of Fonseca and his myrmidons. It was on the deck of his own ship, in the harbour of San Lucar, that he knocked down and soundly kicked Ximeno de Breviesca, Fonseca's accountant, whose nagging requisitions had driven the Admiral to fury.

After all these years of gravity and restraint and endurance, this momentary outbreak of the old Adam in our hero is like a breath of wind through an open window.

To the portraits of Columbus hanging in the gallery of one's imagination this must surely be added; in which Christopher, on the deck of his ship, with the royal standard and the Admiral's flag flying from his masthead, is observed to be soundly kicking a prostrate accountant. The incident is worthy of a date, which is accordingly here given, as near as may be— May 29, 1498.

The End